TOKYO

THE CITY AT

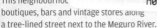

Naka Meguro
This neighbourhood has a string of boutiques, bars and vintage stores along a tree-lined street next to the Meguro River.

Ebisu
An up-and-coming district with the toy-town development Ebisu Garden Place at one end and small shops and cafés at the other.

Atago Green Hills
Architect Cesar Pelli's Forest Tower is a 42-storey residential building providing 354 apartments. The Atago Green Hills development, like Roppongi Hills, is a Mori Building initiative.

Shibuya
Don't miss a visit to the full-on retail experience that is Tokyu Hands, seven floors crammed with everything from notebooks to the wackiest selection of clothes pegs.
12-18 Udagawa-cho, Shibuya-ku,
T 03 3476 5461

Roppongi Hills
After an exfoliation at Adam & Eve (see p092) lose a couple of hours at the art museum atop the Mori Tower (see p012).

Meiji Jingu
This famous Shinto shrine was restored after the original burned down in the Second World War and dates from 1958.
www.meijijingu.or.jp

Shinjuku
The high-rise, high-octane heart of the city is home to one of the biggest railway stations in the world.

INTRODUCTION
THE CHANGING FACE OF THE URBAN SCENE

Tokyo is a city where the details of daily life are all executed impeccably. The tiniest yakitori bars and the sleaziest Shinjuku salons are scrupulously clean. Everything you buy is perfectly packaged. Yet the architectural fabric of the city is almost wantonly neglected. Tokyo's urban landscape only comes alive at night, when the sprawl of concrete morphs into a neon ocean, and the electronic ribbons of car lights lace airborne expressways; but all you see of Tokyo by day is mile after mile of grubbily greige buildings, with clumps of electronic cables tangled between them There is an upside to this. When nothing is permanent, developers take more chances. Philippe Starck's Golden Flame, atop the Asahi Beer Hall (1-23-1, Azumabashi, T 03 5608 5381), might look odd on the banks of the River Sumida, but it's inconceivable to think of it ever having been allowed to be built beside, say, the Seine.

Other aspects of contemporary culture have the same frenzied air. Clubs and bars fall in and out of favour so swiftly that London and New York seem staid by comparison. Tokyo is equally beguiling when it's at its most Japanese. The rough-hewn ceramic urns on the roof of the Mingeikan Folk Crafts Museum (4-3-33 Komaba, T 03 3467 4527) are arranged like an artistic composition. This sort of real-life retro is just as much a part of city life as the pop princesses who tote plastic pistols like fashion accessories when dancing on tables. It's all here and more, just waiting to be explored.

ESSENTIAL INFO

FACTS, FIGURES AND USEFUL ADDRESSES

TOURIST OFFICE
10th Floor, Tokyo Kotsu Kaikan Building
2-10-1 Yurakucho, Chiyoda-ku
T 03 3201 3331
www.jnto.go.jp

TRANSPORT
Car hire
Hertz
T 012 048 9882
Mazda Rent-A-Lease
T 03 5286 0740
Metro
www.tokyometro.jp
Narita Express Train
www.jreast.co.jp
Taxis
Tokyo MK
T 03 5547 5551
Kokusai Kotsu Taxi
T 03 3901 1111

EMERGENCY SERVICES
Ambulance
T 119
Police
T 110
24-hour pharmacy
The American Pharmacy
Marunouchi Building
2-4-2 Marunouchi
T 03 5220 7716

CONSULATES
British Consulate
1 Ichiban-cho, Choyoda-ku
T 03 3265 5511
www.uknow.or.jp
US Consulate
1-10-5 Akasaka, Minato-ku
T 03 3224 5000
www.tokyo.usembassy.gov

MONEY
American Express
2-5-1 Yurakucho, Chiyoda-ku
T 03 3286 5620
www10.americanexpress.com

POSTAL SERVICES
Post Office
5-14 Shinsuna 3-chome, Koto-ku
T 03 5665 4130
Shipping
UPS
T 120 27 1040
www.ups.com

BOOKS
Fruits by Shoichi Aoki (Phaidon Press)
Inventing Japan by Ian Buruma
(Phoenix Press)
Tokyo: A View of the City by Donald
Ritchie (Reaktion Books)

WEBSITES
Architecture
www.japan-architect.co.jp
Art/Design
www.pingmag.jp
Newspapers
www.tokyo.to
www.japantimes.co.jp

COST OF LIVING
Taxi from Narita Airport to city centre
€205
Cappuccino
€3.40
Packet of cigarettes
€1.70
Daily newspaper
€1
Bottle of champagne
€65

TOKYO
Area
2,187 sq km
Population
12.5 million
Currency: yen
¥100 = £0.47 = €0.68 = $0.86
Telephone codes
Japan: 81
Tokyo: 03
Time
GMT +9

JAPAN
Tokyo
Beijing
Shanghai
Hong Kong
Bangkok

AVERAGE MAX TEMPERATURE / °C

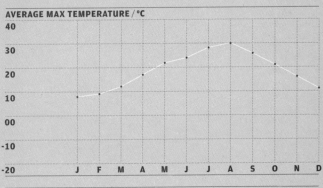

	J	F	M	A	M	J	J	A	S	O	N	D

40
30
20
10
00
-10
-20

AVERAGE RAINFALL / MM

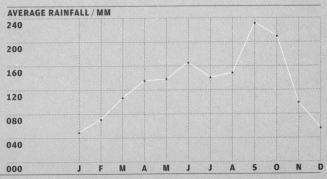

240
200
160
120
080
040
000

	J	F	M	A	M	J	J	A	S	O	N	D

NEIGHBOURHOODS
THE AREAS YOU NEED TO KNOW AND WHY

To help you navigate the city, we've chosen the most interesting districts (see the map inside the back cover) and underlined featured venues in colour, according to their location (see below); those venues that are outside these areas are not coloured.

ASAKUSA
North-east of the city centre, Asakusa is the heart of *shitamachi*, the downtown area. Home to Tokyo's best-known temple, Sensoji, and the cherry blossom-lined Sumida River, the area retains its Edo-era entertainment-district flavour with street stalls, *jinrikisha* (rickshaws) and festivals.

EBISU AND MEGURO
Grown-ups tired of crowds, neon lights and noise should come here, to find a maze of winding lanes lined with Tokyo's best cafés, avant-garde fashion stores and the city's best record shop, Bonjour Records (T 03 5458 6020). Meguro is where Tokyo's intelligentsia are heading right now for retro finds and first-edition books.

GINZA AND SHIODOME
Think shopping and you think Ginza, where every store here is out to be better than its neighbour. You should visit Renzo Piano's glass block-covered building for Hermès, the fibre-optically illuminated Dior building (see p058) and the stately Ginza Wako. Shiodome, which mostly dates from 2000, is a mecca for lovers of skyscrapers.

AOYAMA AND HARAJUKU
Jingubashi (Shrine Bridge) at the gates of the Meiji Jingu shrine sums up Japan's blend of old and new, as just outside Harajuku girls gather to play J-pop. Nearby are architectural gems, such as Tadao Ando's Omotesando Hills (see p077).

SHIBUYA
Tokyo's youth epicentre, home to *gyaru* (think Paris Hilton after three weeks in a tanning machine), *gyaruo* (the male version) and schoolgirl wannabes shopping for size-6 miniskirts and tight tees. The alleyways that criss-cross the major streets are crammed with bars.

SHINJUKU
Shinjuku has everything Tokyo has to offer in one compact area. For fashion, head to Isetan, for architecture, check out the Park Hyatt (see p024), the hotel in *Lost in Translation* and, for a bit of naughty fun, go to Kabukicho, the city's outrageous nightclub, bar and red-light district.

MARUNOUCHI AND NIHONBASHI
All roads lead to Nihonbashi – distances to Tokyo are measured to the area's sadly neglected stone bridge, Nihon Bashi. The area is also home to the Tokyo Stock Exchange and Mitsukoshi department store. Modelled on Amsterdam's Centraal Station, Tokyo Station is Marunouchi's most treasured building.

UENO
Ueno contains fine museums and the city's oldest park. Walking down the shopping street Ameyoko is like stepping back in time. The stalls sell everything from fish to furniture, and the market sellers are said to be the best in the business. Expect to buy far more than you had planned.

LANDMARKS

THE SHAPE OF THE CITY SKYLINE

Each area of Tokyo has its own style – tacky teens head for Shibuya, manga and electronics heads go to Akihabara, well-heeled ladies go to Ginza, for its department stores, pukka kimono and gift shops and, increasingly, designer labels. On Sundays, Ginza's Chuo Dori is closed to traffic and shoppers take to the street.

Marunouchi, the area around Tokyo Station, has been transformed and the once boring business district is now buzzing with beautiful stores and cafés. Can't wait to start exploring? Hold on a moment. For all the media-fed familiarity of the place in recent years, Tokyo – from its inexplicable social mores to a labyrinthine street plan designed by 15th-century warlords to confuse invading enemies – is unfathomable. We've tried to offer you some recognisable structures to help your way around the city, but, at some point, all you can do is drink it in, and let yourself be dazzled by its visual delights. You can check out the cute kanji characters on pastel supermarket packets, and the hallucinogenic riot of fake floral garlands and tumbling silver balls at neighbourhood *pachinko* parlours. And that's before you've ogled the Mori Tower skyscraper (see p012), charged your chopsticks in an excessively expensive *ryotei*, or purred away on the lacy seat of a candy-coloured taxicab after an assignation in the decadent, eat-your-heart-out Eameses, lobby of Hotel Okura (see p022).

For all addresses, see Resources.

Tokyo City Hall

This cathedral-like structure in granite and steel is City Hall, known as the *Tocho*. Built in 1991, it was designed by the influential architect Kenzo Tange and rises 48 floors, splitting at the 33rd floor into twin symmetrical towers. On a clear day, you can see Mount Fuji from the observation decks on the 45th floor, reached by elevator in 55 seconds.

2-8-1 Nishishinju-ku, Shinjuku-ku

Mori Tower

By far the best thing about this 28-acre 'city within a city' complex of high- and low-rise buildings, apartments, shops, restaurants, hotels and offices is the modern art gallery, perched on the top two floors of this 54-storey tower. It should be good – it's personally looked after by the wife of Minoru Mori, Japan's largest commercial landlord and the man who spent decades patiently acquiring this vast site from hundreds of small local landlords. Not only an excellent vantage point from which to get a sense of Tokyo's urban sprawl, when lit up at night it's an unmissable landmark in frenetic Roppongi.
6-10-1 Roppongi Hills, Minato-ku, www.roppongihills.com

Tod's Omotesando Building

In recent years, high-end fashion brands, from Louis Vuitton to Dior, have been queueing up to purchase a patch of Omotesando real estate. For the flagship shop and office of Italian brand Tod's, Japanese architect Toyo Ito took his design cue from Omotesando's towering zelkova trees, and in an uncharacteristic act of Tokyo preservation, the trees have been spared. The concrete exterior of the building is both a tree-shaped silhouette and an integral part of the structure. It certainly stands out among the glass buildings in the area. At the very top of Tod's is a secret eyrie: a meeting/dining room with leather-clad walls and a leather table. Outside is a garden and a terrace – perfect for a spot of people-watching.
5-1-15 Jingumae, Shibuya-ku,
T 03 3797 2370

Caretta Shiodome

The celebrated French architect Jean Nouvel's contribution to the Tokyo skyline is this 48-storey HQ for the advertising behemoth Dentsu Inc. It's fair to say that admirers of this skyscraper, completed in 2002, are rather thinner on the ground than those of the architect's remarkable Quai Branly museum in Paris or Guthrie Theatre in Minneapolis, but what can't be denied is that it makes an imposing presence on the Tokyo skyline. Built over the site of Tokyo's first train station and alongside the Hamarikyu Gardens, this slim skyscraper has dominated the massive Shiodome development in much the same way as the Mori Tower (see p012) does Roppongi Hills. There are 70 elevators and it rises to 213m. There is an observation deck, café and restaurant on the 46th and 47th floors.
1-8-1 Higashi-Shimbashi, Minato-ku
T 03 6216 5111, www.dentsu.com

HOTELS

WHERE TO STAY AND WHICH ROOMS TO BOOK

With international chains piling in, Tokyo's hotel landscape appears to be changing. Recent arrivals include the Conrad Tokyo (see p020) and the Mandarin Oriental (see p028), which will soon be joined by the Ritz Carlton (www.ritzcarlton.com) and Peninsula (www.peninsula.com). Still, classics like Hotel Okura (see p022) and the New Otani (4-1 Kioi-cho, Chiyoda-ku, T 03 3265 1111) have a unique appeal and a strong sense of place. The New Otani opened for the 1964 Olympics and has been a landmark ever since. It functions like a small town, with medical staff, a chapel, a 400-year-old Japanese garden, 1,533 guest rooms and 37 bars and restaurants.

The Imperials still favour, naturally, the Imperial Hotel (1-1 Uchisaiwai-cho 1-chome, Chiyoda-ku, T 03 3504 1111). This Frank Lloyd Wright building was demolished in 1967, and though the lobby now sits in an architecture park near Nagoya, a whiff of history is still evident in its modern incarnation. The Yamanoue, or Hilltop Hotel (1-1 Surugadai Kanda, Chiyoda-ku, T 03 3293 2311), in Jinbocho is another hotel with a long pedigree. Once home to US army officers, the rooms have a charmingly worn mix of Western beds and tatami mats. Japanese business hotels are often a cheaper option, but can verge on the box-like. The Mitsui Garden Hotel in Ginza (8-13-1 Ginza, Chiyoda-ku, T 03 3543 1131), designed by Piero Lissoni, attempts to push them in a more stylish direction. *For all addresses and room rates, see Resources.*

Claska

This 1970s block was revamped by the architects Intentionallies in 2003, and remains the only real boutique property in the city. The nine rooms are a treat, sparsely filled with handcrafted furniture and low-key Japanese touches. No two rooms are the same: one has an attached terrace, another has a view from the bathtub. The first-floor restaurant, The Lobby (see p052), has its own party space, while the second-floor gallery showcases the newest cultural creations. It also has a popular bookshop and the city's trendiest pet parlour, DogMan.

1-3-18 Chuo-cho, Meguro-ku,
T 03 3719 8121, www.claska.com

Room 402, Claska

Conrad Tokyo

Like many of the city's hotels, the Conrad spans the top floors of a tower, this one in the gleaming high-rise district of Shiodome. First impressions are arresting – the entrance hall (above) is adorned with a huge bright red sculpture – while elsewhere, dark wood interiors abound and views, particularly from the Garden Rooms, are spectacular. In-house dining options include two Gordon Ramsay restaurants, Gordon Ramsay at Conrad Tokyo (his first opening in Asia), and the more casual brasserie Cerise, as well as an excellent Japanese restaurant, Kazahana.
1-9-1 Higashi-Shinbashi, Minato-ku, T 03 6388 8000, www.conradtokyo.co.jp

Yoshimizu

Situated in the heart of Ginza, this Kyoto inn is the place to go for the traditional Japanese experience. This serene retreat offers Japanese-style rooms (above), utilising mainly natural, chemical-free materials, such as tatami on the floor and *keisodo* (a porous clay) in the walls. You'll also find traditional *shoji* screens and futon mattresses. If you've had a hard day's shopping round the upmarket shops in the area, the cedar and stone baths are perfect for recuperating, before you sample the local organic food from the hotel's restaurant.

3-11-3 Ginza, Chuo-ku, T 03 3248 4432,
www.yoshimizu.com

Hotel Okura

Modernist architecture buffs adore this
1962 Yoshiro Taniguchi hotel. The public
spaces have been spared renovation and
the lobby (pictured) is the most elegant
in Tokyo. If money is no object, book the
Imperial or Presidential Suite – usually
reserved by heads of state – which
remain just as they were 40 years ago.
2-10-4 Toranomon, Minato-ku,
T 03 3582 0111, www.okura.com/tokyo

Park Hyatt

The un-named star of *Lost in Translation*, this luxury hotel, known for its stellar service as well its clientele, was already the first choice for many visitors to Tokyo. Perched on the top 14 floors of a giant 52-floor Shinjuku skyscraper, the hotel's striking nature is evident on arrival, when guests are met in the spacious lobby (above) by a looming piece of modern art. The Park Hyatt has some of the largest and most tech-filled suites in the city, as well as a vertiginous indoor swimming pool, a newly renovated spa and the relentlessly popular New York Grill & Bar. For picture-perfect vistas across to Mount Fuji, ask for a Park View King Room.
3-7-1-2 Nishi-Shinjuku, Shinjuku-ku
T 03 5322 1234,
http://tokyo.park.hyatt.com

Sofitel

Inspired by both traditional Japanese temples and, apparently, also by the Tree of Life, the 26-storey, 83-room Sofitel was designed by Kiyonori Kikutake, a local architect who is best known for the uncompromising Edo-Tokyo history museum (www.edo-tokyo-museum.or.jp), and opened in 1994. In truth, the hotel is probably better enjoyed from without than within, and there is nothing special about the rooms, but the service is good and the hotel offers suitably high-tech business facilities. The location, near Ueno Park in the Taito district, is another plus.

2-1-48 Ikenohata, Taito-ku, T 03 5685 7111, www.sofitel.com

Four Seasons Marunouchi
The Marunouchi district has blossomed
in the last two years, and what was once
a staid business area is now humming
with fashion stores and restaurants. The
current queen of the crop is this deluxe,
boutique-style hotel inside a glass-clad
skyscraper that overlooks Ginza and
Tokyo Station. Small by Tokyo standards
(it has a mere 57 rooms) the style
here is all neutral palettes with luxe
contemporary touches. The seventh-floor
guest lounge (above) is a comfortable
place to relax and rooms, as you'd expect,
are spacious and modern. We like the
one-bedroom suites, with their guest
powder rooms and egg-shaped tubs in
the bathrooms (right). The package is
completed with a smallish Japanese spa
and a newly relaunched bistro.
*Pacific Century Place, 1-11-1 Marunouchi,
Chiyoda-ku, T 03 5222 7222,
www.fourseasons.com/marunouchi*

Mandarin Oriental

Opened in March 2006, Tokyo's latest luxury hotel has contemporary interior styling by Reiko Sudo, famous in Japan for her textile company Nuno. All rooms come with a view, of course, but are also a gadget-lovers delight, with LCD televisions in the bathrooms and an entertainment system that you can plug your iPod into. If you're not staying at the hotel, stop by for a dim-sum lunch at the weekend, or head up to the 38th-floor lounge (above), where afternoon tea is served before spectacular views.

2-1-1 Nihonbashi Muromachi, Chuo-ku,
T 03 3270 8800,
www.mandarinoriental.com/tokyo

Grand Hyatt

This popular hotel is situated in the mega-development that is Roppongi Hills. And it's a whopper itself: nearly 400 rooms and eight restaurants, plus a round of banqueting rooms and an extraordinary wooden wedding chapel. Highlights include the beautifully low-lit swimming pool and super-sized bathrooms. For those who don't want to share the facilities, the Presidential Suite (above) comes with its own pool, a private terrace, two bathrooms, a kitchen and dining facilities for eight.
6-10-3 Roppongi Hills, Minato-ku, T 03 4333 1234,www.grandhyatttokyo.com

Pool, Grand Hyatt

24 HOURS

SEE THE BEST OF THE CITY IN JUST ONE DAY

There's no reason why a single day in Tokyo can't serve multiple functions. Part of it, perhaps a large part, can be used for shopping, to find things that you simply won't elsewhere; another part, to recharge yourself; and the rest, to sample an enchanting bar and some of the best food to be had anywhere. An early start should see you pounding the perimeter path around the Imperial Palace with the city's well-heeled jogging faithful. That way, you'll earn a spa treatment at the chic new Mandarin Oriental hotel (opposite). Then, you have some serious shopping to do.

While Harajuku and Daikanyama, with their fashion stores and cafés, are worth a visit, the trendsetters have moved to Meguro. Once a quiet, residential area interspersed with the odd art supply store, dressmaker or noodle shop, there is now a mix of boutiques, bars and vintage stores compactly lined up along the tree-lined roads next to the slender Meguro River. Walk along Meguro Dori for some of the best furniture and design stores in Tokyo. Then, there's time for a late lunch, before an afternoon given over to culture and a return to Meguro for a last look around, followed by dinner at Higashi-yama Tokyo (see p038). If you've still got some energy, now is the time to tackle the New York Grill & Bar at the Park Hyatt (see p024). Be advised, though: the clientele here tends to look more like Bill Murray than Scarlett Johansson.

For all addresses, see Resources.

09.00 Mandarin Oriental Spa
Should your hotel not have a particularly
appealing spa area, it's worth knowing
that this new temple to wellness also
welcomes non-residents. One of the most
lavishly appointed spaces in the city,
it has inarguably the best views. Book
one of the private spa suites and you
might feel you're seeing more than
enough of the city from the comfort of
your massage bed up on the 36th floor

to actually bother with venturing out
on to the streets below. It's been popular
since it opened, so book well in advance.
There are generous discounts available for
regular customers.
*2-1-1 Nihonbashi Muromachi,
Chuo-ku, T 03 3270 8800,
www.mandarinoriental.com/tokyo*

11.00 Meguro Dori

Meguro Dori is now known as 'Furniture Street', thanks to the proliferation of mid-century furniture and design stores. Browse the section between the Yamate Dori crossing and the Claska hotel (see p017). Favourites include Acme (T 03 5721 8456; right), for imported American pieces, Fusion Interiors (T 03 3710 5099), for items from Scandinavia and – the best of the lot – Meister (T 03 3716 2767), for classic and modern Japanese design. Other stores to watch out for in the area include Carlife (T 03 5784 0932), which offers a snapshot of women's style in Tokyo, and Cow Books (see p080), which specialises in progressive works from the 1960s and 70s, plus a selection of mint-condition magazines and art and design books. Higashiya (T 03 5720 1300) is a stunning store selling traditional Japanese bean sweets. It's worth buying something here just for the exquisite wrapping.

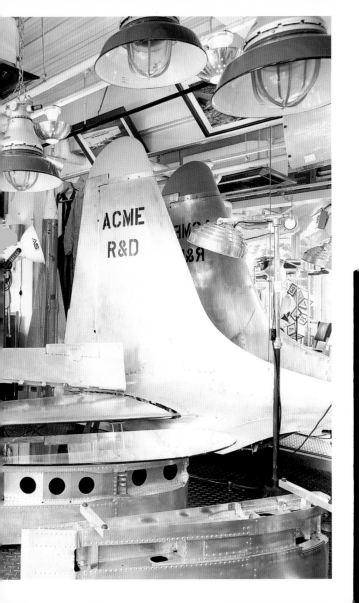

14.00 Maisen

If you have a taste for *tonkatsu*, the delicious deep-fried pork cutlets that are unquestionably worth visiting Japan for, there is really only one place to visit. At Maisen, queues form at all hours of the day, as people wait patiently to devour its set meals of pork *tonkatsu*, organic cabbage, pickles and rice. This Tokyo institution also sells a small range of products, including the sublime *tonkatsu* sauce itself, which, naturally enough, comes in needlessly chic packaging. It's well worth stocking up with a batch to satisfy friends, family and your own *tonkatsu* withdrawal symptoms once you return home.

4-8-5 Jingumae, Shibuya-ku,
T 03 3470 0071

16.00 Gallery of Horyuji Treasures
Designed by Yoshio Taniguchi, now
chiefly celebrated for the new MoMA
building in New York, this is the Tokyo
National Museum's hidden gem.
Tucked away behind the main buildings,
it's worth a look for its stark but serene
architecture. Inside, you can see a
selection of treasures from the Horyuji
Temple in Nara, one of the most
important temples in the country.

The exhibits avoid the over-elaborate
presentation that is evident elsewhere,
and the 1999 building is also a beautifully
understated place to linger. Last admission
is usually at 4.30pm, but the museum
opens until 8pm on Fridays in the summer.
13-9 Uenokoen, Taito-ku, T 03 3822 1111,
www.tnm.go.jp

21.00 Higashi-Yama Tokyo
For traditional Japanese food with
a modern twist, Higashi-yama is
a favourite. The striking interior was
designed by owner Shinichiro Ogata,
whose design studio Simplicity
is also responsible for the tableware.
Roundoff your meal with a drink
in theelegant downstairs lounge.
*1-21-25 Higashiyama, Meguro-ku,
T 03 5720 1300, www.simplicity.co.jp*

URBAN LIFE
CAFÉS, RESTAURANTS, BARS AND NIGHTCLUBS

Eating out is one of the great pleasures of a visit to Tokyo. Japanese cuisine itself is represented in everything from cheap and cheerful noodle bars to high-end *kaiseki* restaurants, where carefully sourced ingredients are prepared and served with meticulous detail. But other nationalities are well represented too, and Tokyo has some fine French and Italian cooking. The great Tokyo bargain is lunch – restaurants that are unapproachably expensive at night often serve a reasonably-priced meal during the day.

Locating restaurants can be problem. Even the best ones can be hidden in the upper floors of an anonymous-looking office building or marked by nothing more than a simple curtain, a red lantern or a tiny sign written in Japanese characters. You may want to call ahead and ask them to fax you a map. On Friday nights, office workers pour into one of the city's thousands of *izakaya* – the equivalent of a pub, but with better food. There are cheap and cheerful standing bars, or plush places with sky-high views and cover charges to match. Music venues range from Ageha (2-2-10 Shinkiba, Koto-ku, T 03 5534 2525), the megaclub in Tokyo Bay, to small venues such as the Blue Note (Raika Building, 6-3-16 Minamiaoyama, Minato-ku, T 03 548 0088) in Aoyama. If you're out all night and looking for an early breakfast, try the sushi bars at the Tsukiji fish market – catch it before it goes.

For all addresses, see Resources.

Restaurant Tanga

The business district of Akasaka used to be filled with *ryotei*: discreet, upmarket restaurants favoured by politicians and executives for private meetings. Restaurant Tanga is built on the site of a former distinguished *ryotei*. Designed by Masamichi Katayama, its reincarnation is pure glamour, from the lobby to the low-lit bar. Katayama has upped the drama with glass floors and ceilings, and rows of lamps. Just visible behind a giant, net-draped wall of glass is the two-storey kitchen, where Masa Nagasaka – one of the first chefs to introduce Californian cooking to Japan – is in charge. In a nod to its past life, Tanga has three private dining rooms, including the Krug and the Wakabayashi, named after the old *ryotei*. *Wakabayashi Building, 2-8-5 Akasaka, Minato-ku, T 03 5575 6668*

Rakusho Kushu Maru
Owner and head chef Keiji Mori spent
10 years honing his culinary skills in
Kyoto, before opening this cosy restaurant
in Aoyama. The menu changes according
to the season. Staples include *goma
dofu* (sesame tofu) and *kamo manju*
(a traditional Kyoto bun made with wild
duck and lily bulbs). The simple chicken
with salt and *yuzu* pepper is delicious. This
place is perfect if you want to try serious
Japanese food without going to the
formality and expense of *kaiseki* dining.
There are a range of simple set dinner
options and a menu in English should you
wish. The warm wooden interior is very
welcoming, and there is a row of counter
seats if you want to get closer to the
young cooking team at the heart of the
action. There are also three attractive
private rooms for small groups.
*Aoyama KP Building, B1st Floor, 5-30-8
Jingumae, Shibuya-ku, T 03 6418 5572*

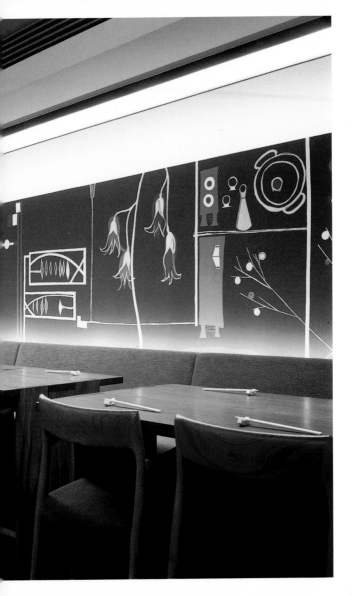

Waketokuyama

Everything about this Kengo Kuma-designed restaurant speaks of immense care and attention to detail, from the tradmark steel louvres that shade the exterior of the building from the hubbub of the street outside to chef Hiromitsu Nozaki's delicate, seasonal Japanese cooking. He has built up a fiercely loyal following with his emphasis on quality ingredients. The set dinner he serves in the evening, although emphatically not cheap, is usually booked up for weeks in advance. If nothing else, his signature dessert dish, featuring broad beans, oranges and black honey, will restore your faith in the power of human creativity.
5-1-5 Minami-Azabu, T 03 5789 3838

Wired

Internet cafés are few and far between in Tokyo, as most people have access through their mobiles. If you're passing through and find yourself in need of a quick browse, look out for the chain of Wired Cafés, which offer free access. The latest, Wired Café News, has a bank of laptops, plus wireless access, and you can enjoy pasta, salad and rice dishes followed by a green tea sundae while you surf. There are also cosy sofas, where you can catch up on the week's news in print or via the wall-mounted televisions. *2nd Floor, Mitsui Tower, Nihonbashi-Muromachi, Chuo-ku, T 03 3231 5766, www.cafecompany.co.jp*

Beige

In Tokyo, it seems, nothing succeeds like excess. Perched atop the new Chanel building in Ginza, and named after Coco's favourite hue, this French restaurant is backed by celebrity designer Karl Lagerfeld, catered by celebrity chef Alain Ducasse and designed by celebrity architect Peter Marino. It should all be far, far too much. Consider also that Ducasse's menu liberally mixes the richness of ingredients such as foie gras and lobster with the more delicate flavours of Nemuro scallops. In fact, it's much better than that all makes it sound. True, the hype meant that Beige got 2000 bookings before it opened, but it has been the quality of the cooking and the surprisingly relaxed atmosphere that keeps the good-looking regulars coming back.

10th Floor, Ginza Chanel Building,
3-5-3 Ginza Chuo-ku, T 03 5159 5500,
www.beige-tokyo.com

X+Y

Named after Naomi Chiaki's classic
track 'X plus Y = Love', and part-
designed by cult photographer Kyoichi
Tsuzuki, this bar is like no other in Tokyo.
The glitter ball, white baby grand
and a dark alcove lined with saucy nudes
(above) completes the retro feel, while
the soundtrack is Japanese 60s and 70s.
*4th Floor, Yoshikawa Building, 1-4-11
Ebisu-nishi, Shibuya-ku, T 03 5489 0095*

Kurage

A busy café in the Shibuya Workers' Welfare Hall, this building was spruced up in 2005 with the addition of Kurage and a new branch of the government-run art space, Tokyo Wonder Site. The Deli Lunch especially is a bargain. For ¥840, you can choose from a selection of Japanese dishes – regulars include fried lotus root and prawns, chicken and burdock salad, and sweet pork and egg – which all come with miso soup, five-grain rice and pickles. There's also a full drinks menu. Kurage is open until 11.30pm.
1-19-8 Jin'nan, Shibuya-ku

Toraya Cafe

Confectioner Toraya has been making bean-paste delicacies for centuries. Its key ingredient is the adzuki bean, which it uses to make traditional Japanese sweets and to concoct a whole host of fusion cakes, such as its justly celebrated bean, chocolate and rum gateau. It should be said that Toraya has become a bit of a theme-park experience and you should definitely expect long queues at the weekends, but no one's delicacies are quite as, well, delicate, as those at this Tokyo institution.

6-12-2 Roppongi-keyakizaka Dori, Roppongi Hills, tel 03 5786 9811

The Lobby

The spacious lobby bar at the Claska
hotel (see p017) makes a particularly
good stop after a hard day scouring
the design stores in the Meguro district
(see p034 for our shopping suggestions
there). Check out the DJs and the good-
looking crowd or just enjoy architect
Shuwa Tei's winning way with wood.
1-3-18 Chuo-cho, Meguro-ku,
T 03 5773 8620, www.claska.com

INSIDER'S GUIDE

MAYU YOSHIKAWA, TEXTILE DESIGNER

Yoshikawa, who works for Japanese designers like Issey Miyake, might begin a post-shopping evening with a drink at the Montoak bar and café (6-1-9 Jingumae, Shibuya-ku, T 03 5468 5928), designer Ichiro Katami's relaxed retreat from the wall-to-wall designer shoping of Omotesando. If it is a more formal affair, her choice might be the Orchid bar at Hotel Okura (see p022). This is a bar that evokes the glamour and the gravitas of Japan's post-war power brokers and, importantly for a designer, the graphics are pretty good as well.

For food, she heads to Adan (5-9-15 Mita, Mita, T 03 5444 4507), which has Okinawan cooking from the south of Japan and live music, all presented in a traditonal Japanese-style warehouse setting with cute wooden furniture. For tapas and flamenco, she goes to Las Meninas (2nd Floor, 3-22-7 Koenji Kita, Suginami-ku, T 03 3338 0266) in hip Koenji. Her late-night drinking spot is the tiny Red Bar (1-12-22 Shibuya, Shibuya-ku), best-known for its hundreds of chandeliers. 'It's always fun, and so small you feel as if you're drinking in a packed train,' she says. For clubbing, she heads to Ageha (2-2-10 Shinkiba, Koto-ku, T 03 5534 2525), a giant venue with an outdoor pool. To recover from the night before, Yoshikawa suggests an early breakfast at Tsukiji fish market, and as an adventurous escape from the city, the 10-hour boat ride from Tokyo Bay to Hachijojima, one of the city's outlying islands.

ARCHITOUR

A GUIDE TO TOKYO'S ICONIC BUILDINGS

The combination of a huge earthquake in 1923 and fierce bombing during the Second World War has left few old buildings in Tokyo, and what did survive has largely been flattened by developers. Tokyo is in a constant state of flux – and construction – and visitors can feel overwhelmed by the sprawl of expressways and buildings. Until recently, the threat of earthquakes kept the city low-rise, but now engineering allows it, Tokyo is building skywards, changing the landscape with vast developments such as Roppongi Hills.

For a condensed guide to contemporary architecture, take a walk down Omotesando, where an array of 'starchitects', including Tadao Ando, Kazuyo Seijima, Kisho Kurokawa, Toyo Ito and Jun Aoki have produced flagship stores for the big designer labels. Traditional architecture is increasingly hard to find, but there are unexpected gems, such as the Mingeikan (4-3-33 Komaba, Meguro-ku, T 03 3467 4527), the folk crafts museum founded by Soetsu Yanagi, housed in a beautiful 1936 stone and stucco building with a wooden interior and tiled roof. Anyone interested in old Tokyo should head to the Edo-Tokyo Open-Air Architectural Museum in Koganei City (3-7-1 Sakura-cho, T 042 388 3300), which has an impressive collection of buildings, all saved from demolition by developers and relocated to a suburban park – from wooden *minka* farmhouses to flower shops, private homes and bathhouses.

For all addresses, see Resources.

Tokyo International Forum

This giant cultural complex was designed by Uruguayan architect Rafael Viñoly and completed in 1996. The project includes four auditoriums of various sizes and a central public concourse, but its most striking feature is a 210m-long oval glass hall, which hugs the railway tracks linking Tokyo station with Yuraku-cho. For a bird's-eye view, take a peek from the nearby Four Seasons hotel (see p026), which is also located in the office district of Marunouchi. Part of the vast area that the Forum now inhabits was once occupied by Kenzo Tange's first City Hall building.
3-5-1 Marunouchi 3-chome, Chiyoda-ku,
T 03 5221 9000

Dior

Designer labels are competing with each other to build increasingly lavish Tokyo stores, mostly along Omotesando, the city's best-known shopping street. Avant-garde favourite Jun Aoki built Louis Vuitton's biggest store there, inspired by a pile of the label's luggage (takings on the first day reached $1m); Toyo Ito designed a new Japanese flagship for Tod's (see p013), and just down the road in Aoyama, Herzog & de Meuron's glass honeycomb Prada store is now a Tokyo landmark (see p069). And that's not including remarkable stores by Renzo Piano for Hermès and Shigeru Ban for Swatch in Ginza. Kazuyo Sejima and Ryue Nishizawa designed this stunning transparent tower (above) for Dior.
5-9-2 Jingumae, Shibuya-ku,
T 03 5464 6263, www.dior.com

St Mary's Cathedral

Kenzo Tange is one of the great names in modern Japanese architecture. He designed St Mary's in 1964 to mark the centenary of Japan's official recognition of Catholicism. The original building had been destroyed in 1945, and Tange replaced it with this structure, based on the metaphor of a bird with open wings.When seen from above, the church takes the form of a cross. Although the dramatic exterior is the real show-stopper, the skylight and a window positioned behind the altar create an interesting interplay of light and dark inside the church.

3-16-5 Sekiguchi, Bunkyo-ku

Roppongi Hills
Opened in 2003, this $2.5bn shopping,
residential and office complex in
Minato-ku attracted 49 million visitors
in its first year. American architects
Kohn Pedersen Fox designed the
central building, Mori Tower (see p012).
Other landmarks include Fumihiko
Maki's headquarters for TV Asahi
and Tatsuo Miyajima's giant light
installation (pictured).

Bunka Kaikan

Designed by modernist architect Kunio Maekawa in 1961, to celebrate Tokyo's 500th anniversary, Bunka Kaikan (or Metropolitan Festival Hall) is his most famous work. Regarded as one of Japan's top 20th-century architects, Maekawa began his career in the 1920s, working for Le Corbusier in Paris and returning to Japan in 1930. Bunka Kaikan, in Ueno Park, comprises a concert hall, recital hall, rehearsal rooms and a music library. Not only is the interior much-loved by fans of Japanese modernism, Maekawa was a music buff himself, and collaborated with technicians to give the hall its celebrated sound. Maekawa died in 1986. His house – another of his great works – is preserved in the Edo-Tokyo Open Air Architectural Museum (see p056).

5-45 Ueno Park, Taito-ku, T 03 3828 2111

National Yoyogi Stadium

Kenzo Tange's stadium complex for the Tokyo Olympics in 1964 is regarded as his greatest achievement. Wedged between the busy districts of Shibuya and Harajuku, it is a notable city landmark, and the main building has been compared to everything from a seashell to a Japanese temple. The 1964 Olympics were a key turning point for post-war Japan, and a pivotal moment in Japanese design. Look out for the nearby bridge, emblazoned with sporting motifs, and the Olympic apartments, which are still at the top end of Omotesando, then check out the stadia in Komazawa park (overleaf). Tange, who was born in Osaka in 1913 and died in 2005, is also remembered for designing the beautiful Peace Centre and Peace Park in the devastated city of Hiroshima.

2-1-1 Jin'nan, Shibuya-ku

Komazawa Park Olympic Tower
The full extent of Tokyo's architectural bounty from the 1964 Olympic Games wasn't restricted to Tange's Yoyogi stadium and environs (see p063). Modernist pioneer Mamoru Yamada added a fabulous martial arts centre in Kitanomaru Park, while over in Komazawa Park, Yoshinobu Ashihara contributed an impossibly elegant sports complex, with a wonderfully sharp-angled roof. Masachika Murata trumped that with this football stadium with a curved projecting roof, adding a sharply geometric tower at its entrance, intended to stand as a bold reminder of the success of the Games.
1-1 Komazawa-koen, Setagaya-ku

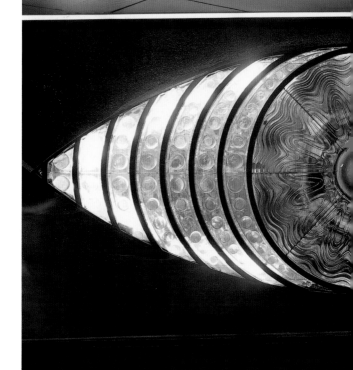

The Eye of Shinjuku
Yoshiko Miyashita's weird and
rather wonderful artistic set piece
has been a Tokyo staple since 1969.
However, despite its prime position,
directly facing Shinjuku Station's
western exit, it is usually ignored,
or else simply overlooked by hurried
salarymen commuting through the
frenzied madness.
Shinjuku Station, Shinjuku-ku

Baisoin Temple

Think Japanese temples and you tend to think ancient wooden buildings, billowing incense and ageing moss gardens. In which case, Kenzo Kuma's 2003 Baisoin will come as a shock. In central Tokyo, a stone's throw from the most fashionable streets, it is the face of modern Buddhism: a modern, multi-storey temple, with attached offices and apartments. There had been a temple at this location for about 350 years, but the priest decided to demolish the original temple and called in Kuma to redevelop the site. The front (above) is shaded by Kuma's signature slender steel louvres.

2-24-8 Minamiaoyama, Minato-ku

Prada Aoyama

Swiss duo Herzog & de Meuron designed this glass honeycomb for Prada on a narrow street in upmarket Aoyama. Designer stores are thick on the ground around here, but all pale in comparison. By day, architecture students flock to gaze; by night, it glows like a lantern. Inside, it is pure luxury, from the thick white carpets to the furry clothes rails and what are Tokyo's most luxurious changing rooms. For a compressed tour of contemporary Japanese architecture, you could do a lot worse than strolling from this shop at one end of Omotesando to Tadao Ando's Omotesando Hills (see p077) at the other.

5-2-6 Minamiaoyama, Minato-ku,
T 03 6418 0400, www.prada.com

National Museum of Western Art
Ueno Park is home to various museums,
including this one, designed by
Le Corbusier, but completed in 1959
by three of his Japanese students:
Kunio Maekawa, Junzo Sakakura and
Takamasa Yoshizaka. Most admirable
is the double-height gallery showcasing
the gallery's 19th-century collection.
7-7 Uenokoen, Taito-ku, T 03 3828 5131,
www.nmwa.go.jp

SHOPPING

THE CITY'S BEST SHOPS AND WHAT TO BUY

Shopping in Tokyo is all about superlatives – the politest service, the most immaculate displays, the best wrapping; luckily, the 'most expensive' tag is not so justified anymore. For fashion, head straight to Aoyama, where you'll find upmarket Japanese labels, such as Issey Miyake, Yohji Yamamoto and Comme des Garçons, plus Herzog & de Meuron's landmark Prada (see p071), before moving along Omotesando to Harajuku, home of the obscure trainer. The side streets are well worth exploring; cult brand Kurachika Yoshida (5-6-8 Jingumae, T 03 5464 1766), behind the Tokyo Union Church (on Omotesando), has the best bags, wallets and luggage.

Go to Daikanyama in Shibuyu-ku for boutiques such as Bonjour Records (24-1 Sarugaku-cho, T 03 5458 6020), a well-edited record store, and Hacknet (1st Floor, 1-30-10 Ebisu-nishi, T 03 5728 6611), an excellent design bookshop. Even Marunouchi is now buzzing with stores and cafés. Beams House (Marunouchi Building, 2-4-1 Marunouchi Chiyoda-ku, T 03 5220 8686) is good for clothes and accessories; head upstairs for toiletries from Marks & Web (T 03 5220 5561). Be sure to visit a *depachika*, the subterranean food hall in most department stores: Mitsukoshi (4-6-16 Ginza, Chuo-ku, T 03 5562 1111) gets top marks. If all this opulence becomes too much, head to earthier areas like Yanaka, with its old-fashioned shops selling everything from bamboo pots to rice crackers.

For all addresses, see Resources.

Hhstyle.com/casa

In Tokyo, where retail architecture gets ever more ambitious, it takes something special to make a mark, but Tadao Ando's shop for concept interiors chain Hhstyle. com/casa has done just that. Situated on one of Harajuku's busiest streets, this stops even the most jaded shoppers in their tracks. The origami-style structure, with only a sliver of glass for a shop window, is home to two Italian brands that are in Japan for the first time: Armani Casa, Armani's furniture and homewares line, and Boffi, the kitchen and bathroom brand. The Boffi show kitchens on display are larger than many Tokyo apartments.

6-14-5 Jingumae, Shibuya-ku,
T 03 3400 8821, www.hhstyle.com

D&Department

This shop and café was founded six years ago as an offshoot of design company Drawing and Manual, whose CEO Kenmei Nagaoka had been buying and selling vintage design for years. It is one of the most original places in Tokyo. Located in a 1960s office block, in the obcure, almost suburban, district of Okusawa, it sells an eclectic selection of Japanese furniture and housewares, as well as music, books and second-hand goods. It has always championed 'long-life' design – everyday products that have been on sale for years – and has now turned those low-key classics into into its own brand, 60 Vision, which aims to repackage forgotten items, such as this low-back chair (above), ¥34,650, by A60.

8-3-2 Okusawa, Setagaya-ku,
T 03 5752 0120 www.d-department.jp

Omotesando Hills

World-renowned architect Tadao Ando (see p081) has managed to squeeze a multi-story shopping centre and nearly 40 apartments onto this long slither of land on Omotesando. The result is a retail experience as far from a regular shopping mall as you can possibly imagine – think gently sloping walkways, tinkling ambient music, the daintiest shops you've ever seen and a (well-dressed) mob scene every weekend as visitors crowd in. Shops range from YSL and Bottega Veneta to chic Amadana (see p078) and Delfonics stationery. The restaurants are generally packed, but you can always have a quick *choko* of sake in the Hasegawa Saké Shop, or a tasty bean cake in Toraya Café, one of Japan's oldest confectioners. *4-12-10 Jingumae, Shibuya-ku, www.omotesandohills.com*

Amadana

The architect Shuwa Tei was responsible for the design of the Claska hotel (see p017) and his Intentionallies practice continues to produce award-winning residential and commercial projects. In addition, Tei has developed a career in product design, starting with a range of high-end kitchen appliances for Toshiba. He also created Real Fleet, a company that redesigns and co-brands the most exquisite high-end electronics under the Amadana label. This, the brand's first stand-alone store, offers the full range, including phones, televisions and, unarguably, the most beautiful portable DVD player in the world, encased in laminated bamboo. *B3rd Floor MB316, Omotesando Hills, 4-12-10 Jingumae, Shibuya-ku, T 03 3408 2018, www.amadana.com*

Tendo Ply

Until 2005, the Tendo company, which has been turning out finely crafted plywood furniture for 60 years, didn't have a base in Tokyo. But the Tendo Ply shop, a former dingy prep school transformed into a striking showroom by architect Daigo Ishii, is bringing the iconic brand to a new audience. We've long admired the curvy lines of classic pieces such as Sori Yanagi's 'Butterfly' stool or Mitsumasa Sugasawa's 'Heron' rocking chair (above), and here they are accompanied by a range of accessories, including T-shirts, plywood bins from wood company Saito and Swedish wool rugs.
2nd Floor, 4-35-7 Fuka Sawa, Setagaya-ku, T 03 5758 7111, www.tendo.ne.jp

Corp Aobadai #103
1-14-11 Aobadai Meguro
Tokyo 153-0042 JAPAN

CLOSE ON WEDNESDAY

12:00 - 21:00
We have 1 hour for lunch time

LITERATURE/POETRY
ESSAYS
BEAT GENERATION
BLACK POWER
COUNTER CULTURE
BIOGRAPHY
HUMOR/COMICS
ART
PHOTO
DESIGN/GRAPHIC
ILLUSTRATION
ARCHITECTURE
INTERIOR
MUSIC
HOBBY
NEW SCIENCE
SPORTS
TRAVEL/LIFE
MAGAZINE
FASHION
HISTRY
COOKING
CHILDREN BOOK
CATALOGUE
PAPER COLLECTIBLES
&
FRESH COFFEE

Cow Books
Specialising in obscure books and magazines from the 1960s and 1970s, Cow Books' singularly eclectic selection covers everything from rare printings of beat and Black Power writers to long-forgotten, illustrated and photographic psychedelic treasures. On our last visit, for instance, we picked up a rare first edition of Nobuyoshi Araki's remarkable *Skokuji*, the poignant photo diary of all the food he and his late wife, Yoko, ate together in the last months of her life. The store has a communal reading table, serves good coffee and encourages browsing. As well as two shops in Tokyo, this one in the heart of Meguro (left) and a newer store (T 03 3497 0907) at the Dragonfly Cafe in the midst of Aoyama, there is a travelling bookshop which takes titles on the road.
1-14-11 Aobadai, Meguro-ku, T03 5459 1747, www.cowbooks.jp

Loopwheeler
Named after a type of knitting
machine, Loopwheeler is setting
a new standard in casualware, by
applying bespoke standards to
wardrobe staples. Those in the know
rave about the style and the high
quality of its sweatshirts and T-shirts.
*Yamana Building, B1st Floor, 3-51-3
Sendagaya, Shibuya-ku,
T 03 5414 2350*

Ito-ya

This shop is a stationery lover's dream. The company is now more than 100 years old, and this main branch in Ginza has eight floors of pens, files, cards and notebooks, plus a gallery and tea lounge. As well as the everyday Pilot pens and Camper notebooks, Ito-ya has every possible stationery angle covered, including business-card holders, leather-bound organisers, portfolios and art materials. Don't miss the annex, Ito-ya 3, on a backstreet behind the store, which sells Japanese stationery, calligraphy brushes and handmade *washi* paper. On the ground floor of the annex, there are drawers full of paper printed with traditional designs. To find it, look out for the giant red paper clip on Chuo Dori. *2-7-15 Ginza, Chuo-ku, T 03 3561 8311, www.ito-ya.co.jp*

Bapexclusive

Retail designer Masamichi Katayama has been quietly changing the face of shopping in Tokyo. And when Nigo, the founder of A Bathing Ape, called on him to revamp the Bapexclusive store, he was true to form and totally transformed it. The ground floor (above) is now a stark grid of white tiles with ape-print camouflage on the ceiling. The first floor (overleaf) is the opposite, with a riotous 10-colour carpet and A Bathing Ape shoes spinning around a conveyor belt like plates of sushi. In between is a show-stopping neon staircase, which throbs with shoppers vying to snap up the latest limited-edition trainers and T-shirts.
5-5-8 Minamiaoyama, Minato-ku,
T 03 5772 2524, www.bape.com

SPORTS AND SPAS
WORK OUT, CHILL OUT OR JUST WATCH

Tokyoites work hard and play even harder. On almost any Sunday morning, Tokyo's parks are teeming with toned torsos. Whatever your sport, you'll find an enthusiast here. Namban Rengo (www.namban.org) welcomes out-of-towners for a 40-minute run, starting at the main gates of Yoyogi Park at 9am (8am in summer), every Sunday. While in the park, check out the Yoyogi National Stadium (see p063), designed by Kenzo Tange for the 1964 Olympics, and described by the Pritzker judges as 'among the most beautiful buildings of the 20th century'. Cycling in Tokyo remains a utilitarian pursuit carried out chiefly for the purpose of getting from A to B through the choking traffic. If you're staying at the Claska (see p017), one of our favourite hotels in town, despite an inconvenient location, free bikes are made available for guests.

A trip to Tokyo should take in a sumo bout. Kokugikan, the sumo stadium in Ryogoku (1-3-28 Yokoami, Sumida-ku, T 03 3623 5111) is the place to go. Arrive before noon to be sure of getting a ticket. And, since the 2002 World Cup, football is finding its feet. To see FC Tokyo, head to the 50,000-seat Ajinomoto Tokyo Stadium (T 04 2440 0555), which you'll find in Chofu. If you're looking to unwind, visit Herbes (6-2-2 Minamiaoyama Homes 501, Minato-ku, T 03 3499 5468, www.herbes.co.jp), who'll dip you in a seaweed bath before your 100-minute massage.

For all addresses, see Resources.

歓迎 麻布十番温泉

Azabu Juban Onsen

Visitors without the time for a rustic spa in the country can take a dip in a natural hot spring in the centre of Tokyo. The old-fashioned baths at Azabu Juban Onsen are filled with mineral-rich water from a source 500m below the ground and said to be good for a wide range of ailments. There are segregated and squeaky clean tiled public baths, plus a sauna and the popular tatami relaxation room (above). Some basic Japanese bathing etiquette: wash at the knee-high showers before you go into the bath, and no soap or bathing suits in the water. On most Sunday afternoons, visitors are entertained with traditional songs.
1-5-22 Azabu Juban, Minato-ku,
T 03 3404 2610

Tokyo Golf Club
The members of this club, founded in 1913, marked its 50th anniversary with a new clubhouse (pictured), designed by Czech architect Antonin Raymond. Immaculate and exclusive, this is a members-only club and visitors will require a letter of recommendation from one of the 580 members to play.
Sayama City, Saitama Prefecture, T 04 2953 9111

Adam & Eve

If you like your massages to come with
wind chimes and fragrant oils, then the
utilitarian aesthetic of this bizarre,
boat-shaped spa, opposite the Chinese
Embassy, definitely isn't for you. Adam &
Eve is a segregated, 24-hour, no-nonsense
Korean scrub joint, and devotees swear
by it. Tough masseuses in undies (think
gym mistress not glamour model) set
about you with scouring pads, removing
terrifying amounts of dead skin, followed
by a dousing in cold water. Try throughout
not to make eye contact with the joint's
other habitués, many of whom seem to be
covered in tattoos and to sport bouffant
hairstyles. Once you're done, you can relax
in the hot baths and emerge, glowing
(or possibly rubbed raw) and babysmooth,
then head for a reviving cocktail in the
rather more glamorous Roppongi Hills.
3-5-5 Nishi Azabu, Minato-ku,
T 03 5474 4455

Tokyo Dome
Home to the mighty Yomiuri Giants,
each baseball game here features
dancing furry animals and strong-legged
girls, who pour beer from tanks strapped
to their backs. The venue also hosts pop
concerts, while the surrounding complex
has its own hotel, amusement park and
popular (ie, crowded) spa.
*Suidobashi 1-3, Koraku, Bunyo-ku,
T 03 5800 9999, www.tokyo-dome.co.jp*

ESCAPES

WHERE TO GO IF YOU WANT TO LEAVE TOWN

Visitors to Japan love the novelty of shooting across the country in high-speed bullet trains, but the Japanese, for whom *shinkansen* travel is the norm, hanker after more leisurely journeys. Top of their wish list is the Cassiopeia (opposite), a reassuringly expensive sleeper train that takes 17 hours to make the 1,200km run from Tokyo to Sapporo, on the island of Hokkaido. Okay, so the same journey by air takes 90 minutes and is half the price, but this is an absurdly civilised way to get to some fabulous skiing in Niseko (overleaf; www.niseko.ne.jp), two hours on from Sapporo.

If it's not the skiing season, or what you really had in mind was a complete antidote to the bustle of the big city, Japan is particularly well endowed with places of pilgrimage. Our favourite is Naoshima, an island of stunning natural beauty in Japan's Inland Sea. It's not, it should be said, the easiest place to get to, taking more than six hours by a combination of *shinkansen* and ferry from Tokyo. But ever since Tadao Ando designed its art museum, Benesse House (Gotanji Naoshima, Kagawa, T 087 892 2030), it has been firmly on the global cultural map. In 2004, Ando added a second museum (see p100) on the island, providing an even more compelling reason to visit. Or join the sophisticated weekending Tokyoites as they head to Hakone, and stay at the Prince Hotel (see p102), a 1970s architectural icon in a wonderful lakeside setting. *For all addresses, see Resources.*

The Cassiopeia

All 86 berths in this 12-car sleeper train, which plies between Ueno Station in Tokyo and Sapporo on Hokkaido, three times a week, are graded first class. Designed for two, with either a twin room or a suite, they come with a television, mini-closet, lavatory and the obligatory cotton *yukata* robe and slippers.

A fabulous Japanese or French meal is served in the dining car or in your cabin, and there's a lively after-dinner bar in the restaurant car. The interiors offer luxury, Japanese style – spartan but efficient – and this is definitely the world's cleanest train. Try to book the end suite in Carriage One, which has a panoramic window all to itself. There is simply no better way of heading to the north, for skiing or hiking in Hokkaido (overleaf).

www.jreast.co.jp

Annupuri Mountain, Niseko

Chichu Art Museum

Located on the southside of Naoshima, an island of the Inland Sea of Japan, this museum is built into the headland and barely rises above ground level, so as not to disturb the natural appearance of the site, which is next to a national park. With just nine works in total, by artists James Turrell, Walter de Maria and Claude Monet (a room is devoted to *Water Lilies*), the Chichu's is a select but powerful collection. The concrete corridors that link the galleries, some open to the elements, cleave through the hillside, so the visitor moves from inside to outside, and the sky and the weather become integral to the experience. It's all rather evocative of Ken Adam's Bond movie set designs.

3449-1 Naoshima, Kagawa, T 087 892 3755, www.chichu.jp

Hakone Prince Hotel
Planned by the late Togo Murano,
this perfectly preserved slice of 1970s
architecture sits on the shores of Lake
Ashinoko, a mere couple of hours from
the capital. Hakone is famed for its
cool summer air, hot springs and natural
scenery dominated by the towering
peak of Mount Fuji. So concerned was
the architect to respect the lakeside and
national park setting that he numbered
each tree that was removed during
construction and subsequently replanted
it. Today, the guests are a mixed bunch –
middle-aged couples taking the curative
spring waters, wedding parties, the great
Japanese hotel money-spinner, and
families on multi-generational holidays –
but the hotel is as the architect imagined
it, free from modernisation and fripperies.
144 Moto-hakone, Hakone-machi,
Ashigarashimo-gun, Kanagawa,
T 0460 3 1111, www.princehotels.co.jp